Memoirs of a Rez Girl

Copyright © 2025 by Leslie Crow

All rights reserved. No part of this book may be reproduced, stored in a retrieval system, or transmitted in any form or by any means—electronic, mechanical, photocopying, recording, or otherwise—without the prior written permission of the author, except in the case of brief quotations embodied in critical reviews and certain other noncommercial uses permitted by copyright law.

This is a work of nonfiction. Some names and identifying details have been changed to protect the privacy of individuals. For permissions, orders, inquiries, or to contact the author, please email:
misscrow55@gmail.com

Library of Congress: 2025905467

Paperback ISBN: 979-8-9929163-0-0
Hardcover ISBN: 979-8-9929163-1-7
Ebook ISBN: 979-8-9929163-2-4

First Edition: 2025
Written on the Rez. Printed in the U.S.A.

This book is dedicated to:

Unči,Ína, My Činkši's (Sons),

My Tìwahè (Family),

the Oyatè (People), &

the Wakanyeja (Children).

CONTENTS

Prologue: The Fire Within

Chapter 1: Born of the Land

Chapter 2: Born to Ína

Chapter 3: Two Worlds

Chapter 4: Strength in Motherhood

Chapter 5: Woman with a Chainsaw

Chapter 6: Finding My Identity

Chapter 7: Teacher Life

Chapter 8: The Road to Leadership

Chapter 9: A Journey of Revival

Chapter 10: The Future

Epilogue: The Fire Stays Lit

Prologue

The Fire Within

I have walked through fire. The kind of fire that rages through the pines, where the ash falls above you like snow, and the gray smoke washes out the blueness of the sky. Pulaski in hand, I have stood at mountain peaks overlooking the wonders of all creation, face blackened with sweaty soot, continuously scraping the land to the dirt trying to keep the flames from swallowing everything in their path. I have fallen knee deep into ash pits feeling the unseen heat on my skin, slept night after night in the raw forces of nature, and know that a fire's existence does not care who you are—it only knows how to consume.

I have also walked through the fire of life. The kind of fire that comes with being born an Indigenous female in the desolation of the Reservation. The kind of fire that burns quietly that does not leave charred forests behind, but instead a fire that transforms the soul.

I have been the little girl who watched addiction steal the ones she loved. I have been the young woman with the audacity to dream and believe I was meant for something more, something bigger. I have been the young single mother, cradling my son in the dark, promising him a life I didn't yet know how to give. I know what it is to feel powerless. I know what it is to be told, in ways both quiet and cruel, that you are not enough. That because you come from a place others see as broken, you will never be whole. *That Rez Girl.*

But I also learned this: fire does not just destroy—it cleanses. It forges. It transforms. I was the little girl striving for a better life. I was the single mother who picked up a chainsaw when they said I couldn't. I am the woman who became an educator in an outdated system that never aligned with our principles as Indigenous people. I am the woman who advocates for the children of my people, so they will never have to doubt their worth. I am still that little Rez girl, born of and molded by the fires of Rez life.

This book is not just about my story—it is for every person who has ever felt lost, who has ever believed they were too broken to rise. It is for the single mother trying to hold her world together with sheer will. This is for the young girl who sees her reflection in mine, for the ones who have been told they *cannot*, but who know, deep inside, that they *must*.

You are not just a survivor. You are a warrior. You are not just what you have lost. You are everything you have become. You are not alone. So walk with me through the flames, and let's rise.

Chapter 1

Born of the Land

I was born when the sky rumbles with rolling thunder and is lit with flashes of lightning. A time on this Earth when rain falls to cleanse the land and begins to renew itself. They say we begin our lives having a universal connection to all that is even before we have words to describe it. I imagine the wind whispering the ancestor's voices, speaking to my spirit new to this world. I am adored and cradled by the elders of my family not knowing how this world will welcome and change me. As a toddler learning to walk, I felt the energy of the ground beneath my toes. Lekši (lehk-she, my uncle) held me in his arms while I stretched my little hands to brush his horse's mane. Each day I grew, each day I made connections to the world around me. When no one was looking, I snatched the horse bridle and took off down the road to meet my family's horses in the pasture.

"Ahtah, check her out. Just learned to walk and she's taking off towards those horses again." Auntie told Grandma while they watched me from the window. The world felt so huge as the space in front of me stretched farther than my little eyes could see. I knew nothing of why this land was sectioned off and what it was supposed to be, what it was supposed to *do* to my people.

"Indian Reservations" were created across the United States to house the remaining of my living ancestors. Mostly women and children who were spared after mass genocide and obliteration of our main source of living, tatanka, the buffalo. This space, the "Rez", we lived in was meant to be and feel like a prison camp for my ancestors long ago, even now, and in our generations to come; but, it was so much more than that—it was a feeling, a rhythm, a heartbeat. It was our home. It was where my spirit experienced the land through simply feeling a living presence under my feet, reciprocating the seasons, receiving the sounds all around, heeding its silences. Living on the Rez meant recognizing that our well being is tied to the earth's wellbeing. When the land thrives, the people thrive.

Whether planting seeds, gathering péjutá (medicines), following animal trails, or simply taking up space between this land and the sky, there is a connection that brings a sense of humility, belonging, and purpose. It's a sacred bond that asks for gratitude and gives healing in return. Even in adolescence, I observed nature in its full element. Growing up in that valley, I knew which direction the wind blew at sunrise; I could feel when it would change direction or gently pause its blow. I understood the coming of dark skies and menacing storms when our horses gathered together. Born of the land, I most appreciated the way the wilderness revealed what was to come.

The House That Held Us

Tucked in that valley on the Rez, our settled home was surrounded by high buttes on one side and trees on the other. It stood by itself away from any other houses or traditional communities. Our home was nothing like the ones I saw on TV, no white picket fence, no two story build. Unči's (oon-chee, my Grandma) house was a small 5 bedroom home, with cement steps leading to the front door. No garage, just a small shed and a long clothes line where bedding swayed with the wind. Unči's house carried the voices of my extended family; my 7 uncles, auntie, my mom, and Unči-we all lived within those walls. Sometimes we had relatives stay with us for extended periods of time until they could get on their feet. Unči rarely turned people away who needed shelter for a while. She would say, "If I had the money, takója (tah-koh-zjah, grandchild), I would build a house so big, all those that needed a home would have a place to stay."

Her kitchen was the center of everything. It always smelled like yeast and warm bread, like frying fish and deer meat. The smell of freshly brewed coffee rolled through the hallway as the sun rose. She ran the house like a general, her voice sharp but loving. Unči moved endlessly about the kitchen, weaving through her cooking, cleaning, fixing, and laughing, calling out, "You boys better get my oil changed. I need that tire fixed too!" My uncles jumped out of their spots on the couch and jetted towards the door. Because when Unči spoke, you listened. Every evening the whole house smelled like food prepared with love… Except when she prepared tániġa (tah-nee-gha, cow stomach or buffalo tripe). Ack! The whole house smelled disgusting! She told us a story of why we ate cow stomach.

"Long time ago our people ate all parts of the animal, left nothing to waste. After all the buffalo were killed it was really hard for our people to survive, especially in the winter time."

Unči scrubbed the off-white, honey-comb shaped sheet of cow stomach in the sink as she continued as if thinking out loud,

"I don't know how those cows got over here, but after they took all our buffalo, we had to use cows instead. We had to make a cow last us a long time...so this tániġa (pointing to it with the nod of her head), it helped us when we didn't have much left. It's how we survived."

I love listening to her stories, her experiences, in awe of her survivalist ways. "Gram, how come it smells like that?" I asked her, pinching my nose shut watching her cut into strips. She smirked and dangled a piece in front of my face.

"Ahhh! It's gonna getch you!" Unči said loudly. I was only about five years old, so I couldn't help but scream from the shock. Unči was like that; she liked to tease and make jokes. She enjoyed laughing and making us laugh. Except this time I didn't laugh. I was so scared of that rubbery, white, hairy-looking strip of meat I began to cry. Unči set down her knife, wrapped her arms around me, "Oh takója, I'm sorry…" She wiped my tears, then took me outside where one of my uncles was getting his small shovel ready to pull a few more turnips out of the ground.

My mother, light-skinned and beautiful, worked endless shifts at the hotel in town. She was a single mother like many Indigenous women on the Rez in the 80's. I sat on the hotel room floor while Mom stretched crisp white sheets over each bed meticulously, smoothing out every ripple, her hands precise and practiced. She was not a half-effort woman. She had a focus in her eyes that made every little detail perfect. Mom did everything with her full heart or not all. Mom and Unči both did everything with a fiery passion and knew how to laugh while doing it.

Mom carried a loneliness she never spoke of. She would tell me how hard it was to live on the Rez being a "half-breed". Too white for the Rez, too Native for the white town. She had the kind of beauty that made people stare, but instead of admiration, it brought resentment. Jealousy can be even more cruel on the Rez. She had learned too often that both Native and white people felt inferior because of her petite frame, high cheekbones, sparkling almond eyes, and an altruistic spirit. I watched and learned what it was like for my mother to try and survive in two worlds. I watched her strive for a better life for my sister and me.

Running Free

Almost everyday I ran barefoot down the dirt driveway past my HeadStart building, dust caked to my ankles, my long hair flowing behind me. The sun bronzed my skin, and I imagined that I could run fast enough to catch the shadows of my ancestors. I imagined their spirits right next to me, protecting me. Sometimes I ventured alone among the vast landscape hidden in the hills, the trees, and the creek. I sensed a presence of those before me when I would get too close to something dangerous.

I learned to love the land as Unči's first born son did. My two-spirited uncle was adept to the wilderness. He would go on long hikes scanning the Earth for various objects-rocks, branches, wildlife. He trekked miles and miles of land feeling that same presence of ancestors all around him. As the eldest grandchild I hiked many miles with him. We walked along the creek searching, finding materials from the past. Arrowheads, turtle shells, eagle feathers- even a few ancient shark teeth from a time when water covered this place. He showed me different things that others would have missed- scrapes on a tree, animal droppings, impressions in the grass, rock formations, exposing all the life that lived near our home. It was exhilarating. Our imaginations mingling the stories behind the objects of our discoveries. He learned about the land in ways most do not. I watched how he moved across the ground with a connectedness most have never known. I felt free. We were free.

The Other Side of the Rez

But the Rez was not always kind. One of my earliest memories was waking up in the backseat of a car gazing up out the backseat window at the dancing leaves of a cottonwood hearing shouting outside. My family was celebrating America's Independence Day by the river while I was sleeping in the backseat. I listened, not yet old enough to comprehend what was happening. As I grew older, I came to understand what was happening. It became a normality. Some nights, I lay beside my baby sister, pulling the blanket up to my chin, listening to the sounds outside my window—the loud voices of relatives gossiping, the hum of a Chevy gliding over the gravel, the muffled shouting of someone too drunk to drive home. I knew what beer smelled like before I was seven. When the front door slammed, my baby sister would wake up wondering where our Mom was and run to the kitchen.

"I'm sorry my girl, mom's drunk. Go back to bed. I'll be there to lay by you in a little bit."

She stepped forward, her hands clenching the dish towel on the fridge door like it was the only thing keeping her standing. I learned early that some things were too big for little girls to fix. As strong as our mother was, she still held a secret inside her that only alcohol could drown out. My mother had a different father than my auntie and uncles. Her dad left when she was just a baby too. Unči went on to marry a man, my auntie and uncle's dad. My mother went to live with *her* grandmother on a different reservation. From then on I always wondered why my mother chose to stay with her grandmother than with her own mom. I wouldn't know why until later in my adult life.

The Stories That Raised Me

When we lived with Unči, she told me stories of the old days, of the Lakota women with steady hands who could set up an entire tipi on their own, their backs unbending. Of the Lakota men who could bring back enough food for an entire village in one hunt. Of the grandmothers who cradled newborns while aunties nursed mothers back to health. Of the fathers who sang their babies to sleep. Of the way people in those villages cared for each other and "chipped in" when a baby was born, grateful to the Creator for blessing the people with a new little soul to cherish. She spoke of a time when our people cared for one another in ways that this world had tried to make us forget.

You knew when Unči was reliving the story she was telling. A fire lit inside her eyes when remembered the language she spoke as a child. Out of nowhere she spoke her language fluently as she did when she was child.

"Takója, ehánni tuwèni otúyačinčin čažèkičiyatapi šni..." After she tasted her language on her tongue once more, she'd translate,

"Granddaughter, in the old days, nobody addressed each other by their names freely. We greeted each other with kinship terms, you know 'tíblo' or 'čuwé', like that." Unči continued as we sat outside her house just feeling, listening, to the world around us. She continued to tell me I was Lakota, that my blood carried the strength of those who fought so we could still be here, a warrior's blood.

Unči also told me about her story, growing up with *her* grandmother who knew how to heal with medicines from the earth, and sang songs the earth still remembered. Unči squinted her eyes as if to bring those memories right in front of her; she'd smile gently and rub her own arm when she talked about *her* grandmother. I was young but I knew she caressed herself that way showing she was missing the touch of her grandmother. Unči would always end her storytelling with, "I want my Lakota name, Takoja. So when she (*her* grandmother) calls me 'home' I can go to her." She told me this, I didn't quite understand all that Unči felt at the time, but I wondered what "home" she was talking about.

The Shadows of Boarding School

Unči also carried something else—a sadness she never said out loud, only in the way her voice wavered when she spoke Lakota to the rare number of those who could speak fluently. Loud sighs of relief emanated from my heart when she had found a rare fluent Lakota speaker like herself. Or how her fingers trembled when she held an eagle plume in her hands. The resilience she had always outweighed the deep sadness and she endured through it all her life.

One day, I asked her why she didn't speak Lakota all the time, why I only heard her whisper it under her breath when she was around the family (Tíwahe). She was quiet for a long time, her weathered hands folded in her lap.

"Because they beat it out of us," she finally said. She never wanted her family to have to feel the pain she went through. I didn't understand at first. She wasn't talking about a person. She was talking about something bigger—something that had stolen more than just words. When she was a little girl, they took her and her sisters away. Men in uniforms came to the Reservation, took the children from their families, and put them in boarding schools far away. She had no choice. None of them did.

"They cut my hair," she told me, her voice heavy with something I didn't yet have words for. "Took my moccasins. Scrubbed my skin raw, like they thought they could wash the Lakota out of me." Our people believe that hair is not just hair. It holds a deep history of identity, strength, and connection to the Creator and the ancestors before us.

    I try to imagine Unči, small and afraid, her long black braids falling to the floor in pieces, her little feet all scrunched up in stiff, ugly black shoes. She seemed leery to continue this story, but she said they whipped her when she spoke Lakota, and at that time that was the only language she knew. They told her our language was dirty, that our ways were wrong. They made her pray to a god that was not ours and punished her when she cried for home. Her baby sister cried through the night at those schools. Almost every night, Unči tiptoed past the night guards to her sister's cries. She would cradle her baby sister in her arms and rock her until sunrise when the nuns came back. My chest felt as if a mound of rocks lay upon my heart after hearing Unči remember those days. Unči told of how she tried to run away several times,

"...But they always caught us," she said. They hurt her in unimaginable ways when they took her back to that school. We listened to the bird's chatter as she continued to speak to me in English. She looked down at her brown weathered palms resting on her lap. We just sat for a moment and listened to those birds speak to one another. She slowly closed both of her palms as if she were holding a long imaginary pipe in both hands. No tears. Just grasping this imaginary pipe with both hands as she gazed upward to the sky and then back at me.

"They tried to erase us Takoja," she said, staring out at the land still clenching the imaginary čanupa (chan-oopa, sacred pipe). "But they couldn't. We are still here, my girl."

I didn't know what to say. I tried to pull from the Lakota words she taught me, but nothing came out of my mouth. I reached for her hand, held it tight as if I could pull some of her pain into my little fingers and carry it for her. That night, as I lay in bed, I whispered Lakota words to myself, over and over, letting them settle in my chest. Making up songs so I could remember them easily.

They had taken Unči's words, but they wouldn't take mine. The history of the Reservation for Unči and my people was very hard, but now it was mine.

"Never forget who you are, Takója," she would whisper, brushing my hair behind my ear, "This world will try to make you forget, but you hold your name in your heart. No one can take that from you."

As Unči sat there in her chair, I moved closer to the ground. I sat between her feet, the place I felt the safest in this world, gliding my small brown hands back and forth through the dirt beneath us. With my finger I made a circle around us then pressed my ear to her leg and wrapped my arms around her calf. I looked up at her gazing almond brown eyes.

"Unči?" I said.

"Yes, Takoja."

"How do you say 'I love you' in Lakota?"

"Teh-chee-hee-lah k-sh-toh...teh-chee-hee-lah k-sh-toh..." Unči would tell me slowly and twice so I could remember.

"Unči, tèčihila kšto," I said to her. She looked down at me, smiled, and continued to brush my hair with her fingers. The golden sky warmed our faces as we sat there just listening to the gentle wind sway the branches of the trees, the birds chirping, some flipping through the sunset.

"Mom! Where's supper?!" one of my uncles shouted to us. I followed her back into the house.

I was in love with stars and listened to Unči's stories of how they guided our family. I whispered Lakota words under my breath, even when the world around me spoke English. No matter where I went, I knew that the land that raised me, the same land that carried the footsteps of those before me—would always call me home.

Chapter 2

Born ofÍna

Ína (my mother) left the Rez to pursue her dreams of becoming a registered nurse. As my mother finished her nursing degree, my siblings and I attended public school just down the road from our apartment. In those first years as a student she sat at the table with mounds of books by her side studying, writing. My brother was just a baby then, and my sister just started school. Her and I would walk six blocks to and from school almost everyday. Although Unči raised my sister as a baby, she came with me and mom to this new city away from the Rez.

It was a good place. Oddly enough, Unči's sister and nephew lived in the same apartment complex as us which made it feel more like home. My sister and I played with our cousins and visited our aunties and uncles. I never realized how helpful it was to have them there with us until now. There was little "culture shock" as one might hear when leaving the Rez into a new city. But it still wasn't a walk in the park. My mother studied and my stepfather, who entered my life at the age of three, worked tirelessly as a construction worker trying to keep us fed and pay bills. Sometimes we barely had enough. I remember asking my mom for some toilet paper because there was none to use the bathroom. She grabbed a few sheets of newspaper, crumpled them up over and over to make them pliable and as soft as she could.

"Here, babe. Use this for now. We will get some on Dad's payday."

Day after day my mother studied. We would catch a ride to the college library and I read books while she studied with a friend there. I loved walking through the tall rows of books, reading each spine, pulling out the book that caught my eye, and flipping through the pages, scanning all the words and pictures. I was in early elementary at the time and most of the words were too complex for me to read, but I brought them back to where my mother sat studying.

"What kind of book did you find, babe?" My mom had a curious smile on her face as she wondered how I could carry books that were as large as her anatomy manuals. I pretended to read each page, skimming with my finger, turning about four pages then moving onto another book. There was something so exhilarating to me being surrounded by so many books, so much knowledge in one room. One day I stood on the second floor balcony of the library, looking out at my mother studying so intently, striving for a better life for her family. I sat down glancing at Ína just to make sure she saw me. Book in hand, I had a vision of all the magnificent things I had seen in each book I picked up. Fashion magazines, journals of medicine, sports, worldly societies and musical history-I loved opening books and picking out the words I could understand and visualizing the books' pictures as if they were real life in front of me. I fell in love with books. As we were about to leave for the evening, the college librarian saw that I had three children's books instead of the normal limit of two. She said,

"Read all three to your mom, okay, honey?"

I played "school" and "restaurant" with my siblings and kept them busy while mom studied. She took breaks to cook for us and get us ready for bed, then she was right back at it. I woke up one night very late in the early morning and she was still studying.

"Mom..." I hugged her because she looked so tired. "Go back to bed babe you have school in the morning. I will be coming to bed soon. My test is tomorrow." Ína guided me back up the stairs to my bedroom, tucked me in, and rubbed my back while she hummed a song until I fell asleep. Ína was beautiful like Unči; she had that same fire in her eyes. The same fire that lit up when grandma spoke her language, Ína had that when she had her head in books.

I was so proud of Ìna. She could have stayed in the disparities of drugs and alcohol on the Rez, but she persevered. She became a registered nurse after my 3rd grade year.

"Babe, you are powerful," she told me, "You can do anything and be anything you want to be."

Ína always told me these things and said I was the reason she fought so hard to leave the darkness that the Rez sometimes has. My mother. My Ína. So strong, yet such a gentle spirit. Our healer.

Ína rose before the sun at 4 am everyday to drive 130 miles roundtrip to start her career as a nurse. After a year of commuting to her new job, we moved to a small town where the Indian Health Service was, a short drive from my great grandmother, a full blood Ihanktonwan Nakota woman. Ína raved over her Unči; she said she was the epitome of strength and wisdom.

"When you were just a baby, my Grandma Sophie bounced you in her arms when you cried. 'Shhhh, there, there. Don't cry, Miss Crow, don't cry.' She hardly spoke any English, but even as a baby she called you 'Miss Crow,'" mom told me. While Ína worked at the IHS, providing quality care to our Ihanktonwan people, helping them heal through her good energy.

I started school in this small town not knowing anyone. I was scared and remembered how the white people at city school treated me. From the moment my parents dropped me off at school, I felt that weight of being different. It wasn't the kind of different that made people curious—it was the kind that made them assume. The kind that made them look at my black hair and brown skin and decide who I was before I even had a chance to speak.

The first thing I noticed was the distinct different groups of kids. The "rancher" kids grouped together, while kids whose parents owned business and had prominent jobs were also the "popular" kids. Then there were the Rez kids, the kids who had the same color skin and hair as me. Luckily on my first day I was welcomed by a Rez girl who smiled at me and told me I could stand by her in line. She had pretty almond eyes and the shiniest black hair. I followed her and her friends from class to class and they invited me to sit with them at lunch.

This school wasn't much different than the public school I attended in the city.

But oddly the notion to make me feel like an outsider was more prevalent than the city school. Just my presence made kids snicker, mostly the boys. There was a boy who kept staring at me. I wasn't sure what to make of it; the next day my new friend told me he had a crush on me. He was wealthy and white, very different from the way I grew up. My new friend giggled as she handed me the necklace he gave to her to give to me with my name on it. I couldn't help but blush. My presence also aggravated some of the teachers; maybe they saw it as having another Rez kid join their class that "wasn't going anywhere in life". When I raised my hand, I could see the surprise flicker across their faces, like they weren't expecting a Rez kid to know the answer. When I turned in my work neatly written and complete, I noticed how they skimmed over my name, how they hesitated before calling on me, stumbling over "Wihanblè S'a (wee-hon-bley-s-ah, Dreamer)" like it was something foreign. I heard the way they talked about "the Indian kids," like we were all the same, like we came from some faraway place instead of just ten miles down the road.

"That one is going to end up like his drunk Dad."

"She's not going to turn homework in, she's raising her siblings."

"Every year the Rez kids hold us back from making AYP."

I felt a heat fall over my body and my face began to turn red. I wanted to scream,

Not me. Look at me. I felt embarrassed for those teachers talking that way about my peers, about me. I knew they weren't talking about me, were they? Not only did I care about my learning, I cared about my classmates and wanted to make friends. Unči taught me to be friendly to people and ask how they are doing. She taught me not to be afraid because someone might need my help and I might need theirs.

  The day I started school some of the wašiču (wah-she-choo, white) boys and girls in my class acted like I was invisible; they joked across the classroom not paying attention to the teacher. It was hard to concentrate, and I really loved to learn. Pencil in hand, books open, I was ready to prove that I was more than the stories they told about us. But no matter how hard I studied, it always felt like I had to prove my worth twice as much; like I had to be perfect just to be seen as good enough.

The Court and the Field

Within the walls of that school I felt ignored. If the days in the classroom made me feel invisible, being in sports made me feel like I was on a mission. I was fast, strong, and determined. Track, gymnastics, basketball—it didn't matter the sport. I threw my whole heart into it, because on the court and on the track, I wasn't just a Rez girl. I was an athlete. A competitor.

Back in the city is where I began my love for track. Our elementary school held a big track meet. I ran the 100 meters, 200 meters, 400 meters, and competed in high jump. While in the final heat of high jump I missed the girls' 200 meter dash, so they made me run with the boys. We got to stand on risers and each time I heard my event, "And in 1st place...Dreamer!" It was the most exhilarating moment of my adolescent life.

Now in this new school as a 7th grader, I felt a fire in my heart to "burn some rubber" on that track. After continuously placing first in middle school events, the high school track coach approached me and offered me a spot on the Varsity track team. This was a rare opportunity. I was silently excited, keeping my eye on showing the Varsity track team I was an asset to their team. They doubted and some ignored me as usual. Until it was time to compete. My debut as a Varsity track runner I placed 6th in the 800 meter out of the 12 high school teams. It was such a good feeling. It was an even better feeling of knowing I didn't need anyone's recognition but my own. Yet it continued. The constant weight of what people expected me to be.

"Rez girls don't know how to play this kind of ball," I heard one of the Rez boys say once when he thought I wasn't listening. "She's left handed, she can't shoot."

I spent hours practicing my shot even after practice was over. I studied plays that I learned to read the defense before they could react. The basketball coach had us doing a defensive drill, shuffling our feet backwards while the opponent tried to protect the basketball. She couldn't get past the free throw line. My coach didn't say good job or anything. He just stared at me like he couldn't believe what he witnessed. The next day we did a similar drill and my opponent got by me. My coach said, "Got Dammit Dreamer, you're fast as hell get there!" In front of the whole team. I was embarrassed, but I did what I have always done, work harder. It made some of the girls on the team despise me at the same time. In their eyes, I wasn't skilled—I was just fast. Just athletic. Just naturally agile, as if my hard work had nothing to do with it.

Gymnastics season came quickly. Living in the city I attended a gymnastics camp where I saw this dark skinned girl and curly long hair. Her muscles in her arms and legs were so defined. She moved so gracefully and bounced so high off the ground when she landed her routine. I wanted to be like her. I loved the way my body felt moving through the air, the way the beam demanded focus, the way I could jump and flip and land with perfect control. But no one ever expected a girl from the Rez to be graceful.

"Do you really want to be a gymnast? You know they wear only a swimsuit showing off their butts," a classmate once told me, eyeing my strong brown legs and broad shoulders.

"You don't even look like a gymnast. You probably don't even know what it's about. You'll get hurt, watch."

Some of the girls had been sent to gymnastics camps since they could walk.

This was my first year actually competing. The flipping, swinging, jumping, and engineering my body to glide gracefully across each event took focus and skill. I was powerful, but yet I was delicate. Skin color didn't matter on balance beams, floor exercise, or uneven bars. The dark skinned girl I saw at camp was the standout on the team at this school...and I came to find out she was my cousin! She pushed me to be better. We pushed ourselves to show the others on the team we weren't just Rez kids. We were athletes. We were gymnasts.

I knew that the only way to prove the doubters wrong was to win. And I won. That winter as a 7th grader, I was the only gymnast to qualify for the State Gymnastics Tournament placing in the top 10 on the balance beam. I couldn't believe it! And by the looks of some of my teammates, they couldn't believe it either.

The Best Friend Who Saw Me

Through the first few years at this new school, there was one person who never saw me as "just" a Rez girl—my best friend, Lily. Lily saw the fire in my eyes when we competed in gymnastics together. She looked different from me and my cousin—blonde-haired, blue-eyed, from a family that had been in town for generations. Her parents had great jobs, and her house was like something out of a book. She was the first person who made me feel like I didn't have to prove anything. Her and I were drawn to each other in a way that didn't need words. Her and her older sisters were very book smart, studying law and medicine in high school. Lilly and I walked to her Dad's restaurant after school together talking nonstop about middle school life.

"Hey, Dreamer, there you are," her Dad would say.

"You girls want something to eat?" Our after school go-to food was turkey club sandwiches, sometimes with their homemade fries. Lily's sisters had this light about them that I didn't see in some of the people on the Rez. They were always so kind and happy. We would eat our turkey club sandwiches, and laugh until our stomachs hurt. We'd have sleepovers, watch movies and cry together. I felt safe around her unlike some of the other kids at school; she was genuine and kind. She came to my house on the Rez once, ate frybread at my kitchen table, and learned Lakota words from Unči, her blue eyes wide with wonder.

She invited me on a family trip; we went to visit her grandparents house and she told me to stay beside her. At first, I didn't understand. Then one day, Lily told me the truth.

"My grandpa doesn't like Indians," she whispered, her face red, her hands twisting in her lap. "He doesn't know you, though."

Like if he only knew me, he'd change his mind. I remember nodding, not knowing what else to do. I didn't cry. I didn't get angry. I just tucked the words away, another small cut to carry with me. Because I had heard it before. I had heard it from teachers, from strangers in stores, from kids at school who thought they were funny. But hearing Lily's grandpa didn't like people like me made it hurt in a different way.

Still, Lily never treated me like I was less. She cheered for me at my basketball games, did homework with me, held my hand when life felt too heavy. She could sense when I wasn't myself. We sat under the balance beam at our gymnastic meet; I was feeling physically overwhelmed, so she told me to close my eyes and lay on my stomach. She used a Reiki healing technique on my body using her energy to heal my overworked and tired back. That was Lily. She didn't understand everything, but she understood me. And sometimes, that was enough.

By the time I was in high school, I had built a name for myself. I was on the Roll of Excellence, top of my class. We were consistently winning in track, starting on the Varsity basketball team, and staying involved in school activities. I had done everything I was supposed to do—everything they said Rez kids weren't supposed to do. But no matter how many trophies I won, no matter how many straight A's I got, I still felt it. The weight of the stereotype. The way both white and Rez people alike still waited for me to fail. I remember being called a "wannabe white" or "an apple" by the kids from one of the tribal schools. They said I was wrong for not wanting to be with my own people at the tribal school and the public school was only using me to win in their sports programs.

In the quiet moments, when I was alone with my thoughts, I wondered if I'd ever be enough not just my peers at the public school, but now the kids who looked like me made me feel bad for excelling. I continually began to realize more and more that maybe I didn't need any of their recognition or approval. Maybe proving them wrong wasn't the goal. Maybe the goal was proving to myself that I had always been more than they expected.

After hearing that, it did feel a little lonelier at this school. I never attended a tribal school and wondered what it would be like. I wondered if I would have to fight to be seen. With all my achievements and having my best friend by my side, I couldn't deny my heart's yearning to be back on the Rez with Unči. It was difficult as a high school student seeing all the Native students transfer back to the Rez school so they could have a chance, a chance to be seen and not scrutinized for their identity. A chance to be themselves, a chance to be enough. It was difficult for us, especially in a place where people despised your accomplishments. I longed for that connection I had when I was a little girl on the Rez. The connection Unči and I had sitting there together in each other's presence revisiting the past. The connection our ancestral healers and warriors once had and how the dark history of colonization had taken all we had known.

I missed connecting with Unči. I had to go back.

Chapter 3

Two Worlds

In my parents home, my siblings and I were safe. Our house was steady. Ína was a nurse, always working, always taking care of the people. My Stepdad became a tribal officer, a man who carried both authority and quiet strength, a protector in more ways than one. We had what most people considered a good family.

Our parents made sure we had what we needed: a roof over our head, clean clothes, hot meals, and our own bedrooms where we could sleep without fear. They told us we were smart, that we were capable, that we could be anything. They made us believe we were more than the statistics, more than the stories people told about Rez kids.

But I was drawn back to the place I was born, the land that raised me. I moved back into Unči's house my junior year of high school, the warmth of her home made me feel whole again. She rose at dawn every morning and made coffee, offering a cup to the relatives who came before us by setting a cup outside while she whispered prayers eyes closed looking skyward. Unči held onto some of the practices her grandma taught her, yet the trauma of the past stuck to our lives like char on a burnt marshmallow.

A few of my uncles still lived with Unči and drank, carrying a trauma no one ever talked about. The boys who showed me how to ride horses and taught me all the parts of their motorcycles would come back to the house with a liquor bottle in hand, ready to pass out to do it all over again the next weekend.

Unči was getting old and her rheumatoid arthritis was getting the best of her. It made her knees swell and her pinky finger permanently curl making it difficult for her to do the things she loved most. She loved using her hands. She prepared the most delicious family dinners; her garden swelled with ripe vegetables that I helped her pick. She embraced her grandchildren endlessly until it was too much for her fingers to handle...

"You're not coming in here! You go take that somewhere else!" Unči would yell. The splitting effect liquor had on my family broke my heart. The yelling woke up Auntie. She jumped in front of Unči yelling and pointing her finger at my uncle who was too incoherent to understand as Auntie raged for him to leave. I watched it all unfold from the living room couch; my eyes took in a view my heart couldn't make sense of. My uncle began to yell back, whipping the almost empty bottle at my Auntie's head. She ducked, glass bottle shattering as it smacked into the refrigerator. The liquor made him a completely different person.

Vividly, I imagined this scene like a fire in the wind drastically changing the calm grass into tall flames. I didn't know what to do at that moment, but I was determined to change it all. All on my own.

A mile down the road from Unči's house was the "housing-a complex of tribally owned houses." Most of my cousins grew up there, some without stable parents. They skipped school, using their laughter to cover the hurt in their eyes. My aunties on my biological father's side carried the weight of trauma so deep it seeped into their bones, making their hands shake as they lit another cigarette, as they poured another drink, as they sat in silence because words had never been enough to fix what was taken from them. We were all Lakota. We all came from the same land, the same ancestral stories. But we lived in two different worlds. I pondered this reality and wondered about the perspectives of my Tíwahé (tee-wah-hay, family), wondering why they didn't see themselves as beautiful and irrepressible as I saw them.

    At home, Ìna reminded me to do my homework before bedtime, and my Stepdad checked in on me after his late-night shifts. Even when they had hard days at work, dinner was on the table every evening. I knew when they had hard days. My parents held so many experiences as a police officer and a nurse. Ìna came home face and eyes red after pulling a double shift. She wiped her eyes and sat silently at the kitchen table staring, trying to make sense of what she had just encountered.

"Mom, what happened? Are you okay?" I asked. She let out a sob she tried to fight back with her words,

"I'm okay my girl...we did everything we could. We did everything we could..." she said slowly. The infant she tried resuscitating didn't make it and made its journey back to the stars. I watched as my Stepdad sat outside on the porch in complete silence, čànlì (chan-lee, cigarette) nestled between his middle and index finger, gazing out at the sunrise lowering his head slowly trying to debrief himself from the fatal car accident that involved a two year old. Ìna and my Stepdad were everyday heroes.

They were my everyday heroes and I am so grateful to the Creator to call them mine.

My parents told me stories of ancestors who survived, of warriors who refused to disappear. They reminded me that our blood carried strength, that no matter what the world threw at me, I had a responsibility to rise above it. I wanted to believe that love and safety could fix everything. Every other month or so, my family would go back to the Rez, and visit extended family. Cousins, aunties, uncles all ready to party to celebrate my family's return. Everything that wasn't normal in our new home, was suddenly and overwhelmingly normal in various parts of the Rez. I noticed how deep the wounds ran and no one ever talked about the dysfunction because no one ever saw it as that. It was the "norm" to let it all come and go like nothing had ever happened, when in fact things did happen. No one ever spoke about any of it. Friday and Saturday were illusions. Sunday was for hangover soup and recovery. In these times of my life, it reminded me of those old time movies where the cowboys offered "fire water" to the "Injuns". Our ancestors were tricked with 'fire water'—something new, powerful, and destructive. It wasn't just a drink; it was a weapon. They handed us fire in a bottle and called it trade. Now it has burned through generations.

The Houses That Held Ghosts

Some of my relatives lived in homes where the curtains never opened and the fridge was mostly empty. Where kids learned to pour drinks for their parents before they learned to tie their shoes. Where laughter came easy when the bottles were full, but silence settled thick when they ran dry.

I rode my bike to the housing to play basketball with my cousins and from one of the open windows of the houses I heard, "Turn that up! That's my song!"

"WOOOOOHOOOOOO!" I always knew when the relatives inside were beyond their alcohol limit. The music blared through the house walls and windows and the relatives inside made their best effort to talk over the bass blasting music penetrating through blown out subwoofers.

I remember watching my uncle stumble across the backyard into Unči's house, slurring his words, trying to see who I was through his glossy bloodshot eyes. Luckily, my brother was awake with me and we helped him to his bedroom.

I saw the way Unči's jaw clenched, the sadness in her eyes, the tired way she shook her head. I wanted to be angry. I wanted to scream, Why do you do this? Don't you see what you're doing to yourself? To us? I knew it wasn't that simple.

Because Unči had her hair cut off in boarding school. Because my uncle was beaten in a similar boarding school for simply being a boy with long hair. Because my auntie's laughter used to be louder and more genuine before she lost her daughter in a car accident just after healing from some of her own childhood trauma. Yet in the rolling hills of the Rez comes the continuous unbroken cycle of impoverished pain.

And on the Rez, historical trauma wasn't just a phrase you threw around in the Indian Health Service's Behavioral Health reception room—it was a shadow that stretched across generations, sinking into people's skin, into their hearts, literally affecting our DNA and nervous systems. With every cigarette (čànlì, chan-lee) drag into our lungs, with every drink seeping into our sacred blood. I hated it. I hated the way it stole the people I loved. The way it made me feel guilty for having a safe home when some of my cousins didn't. The way it made me question whether I could ever truly escape it, or if one day, I'd be pulled into it too.

I learned early how to navigate between my two worlds. At my parents house, I was the Rez girl with good grades, the athlete, the one who "had potential", the one with a future ahead of her. With my relatives on the Rez, I was the lucky girl who knew how to keep quiet when the grown-ups got too loud, who was offered alcohol and weed free of charge in high school.

"Hurry up, come party with us! Don't be acting too good!" Or "My girl…try this, you are family…"

The air smelled of smoke and beer on weekends at relatives' houses. Deep down, I knew I started to realize that I couldn't change them, I couldn't make them sober. I also realized I couldn't live in both worlds forever.

I had to choose which one would define me. And even though the past had its hold on my family, I was determined to be something more. Not just for me. For them. For all of us.

Chapter 4
Strength in Motherhood

High School Relationships can be complicated. Especially when you have suppressed memories; I spent the night with my cousin one night who didn't want to be alone. I found out the hard way why. Her parents came home from a party while she slept in the basement. They brought people home with them. A drunk man had made his way to the basement to my cousin's room while we slept. What I thought was a bad dream, what my actual sleepy reality of a man touching my inner thighs with his large scaly hands. I cried with eyes closed, "No!"

 My uncle heard my cry and walked in and threw the man to the floor. The man dashed up the stairs and out the door. Soon after my parents picked me up, and when my mother questioned me about what happened I told her I didn't know and that nothing had happened. I was scared. And erased it all from my memory. I remember now how much life I had in me, being loud and silly without approval. But after that incident at my cousin's house, I became very quiet, reserved, almost always lost in my thoughts. When things like this happen to you as a child, it creates a pain in you that cannot be described. A pain that carries throughout the rest of your life and changes how you see the world. My subconscious tried to rewrite this trauma by looking for love at an early age. To feel wanted, valued and in control, I fell in love too soon.

Relationships

He wasn't what people expected for me. I was the straight-A student, the athlete, the girl with plans. He was tall, handsome, and charming in a way that made me forget to listen to my gut. He was the type of bad boy my stepfather told me not to date. But he made me feel seen in a way I hadn't before. I would drag our home telephone to my room late at night and talk to him for hours and hours. The first time I saw him give drugs to another person surprised me. I cared for him deeply, and couldn't let that get in between my feelings for him. I thought I could change him for the better. I saw him drunk and on drugs. Then came the cheating and I left. I moved back with Unči and enrolled in the tribal school.

It felt good to be back on the Rez. For some reason the air felt lighter at this school. The students looked like me and said hello as I passed them in the halls.

"Hey, what's up Dreamer?" I heard a familiar boy's voice say. It was my cousin Čètàn (chay-tawn). "When did you come back to the Rez? You've been gone for a while cuz." He hugged me then pushed my head as cousins do. I smiled and gave him a little shove with my shoulder. He hugged me again. He could sense my confidence was low after being in the "white" school for so long and he knew how to fix it.

"Thiiiiiiiis one…Let's go hoop!" he said. I followed him to the gym where the 'hoopers' gathered for the after lunch scrimmage. Both boys and girls were on the court playing the game that I loved. Čètàn was good looking and popular. He was also a standout athlete and held much awards in basketball, boxing, track, football, and dancing.

"Me & Dreamer got next!" Everyone looked at us. I wasn't shy but I wasn't outspoken like my cousin was and I got a little nervous when a bunch of the kids sitting on the bench smiled and walked over to us.

"Thiiiiiis guuuuuuuuuuy!" His friend shook his hand, then looked at me in amazement.

"No way bro, this is the cousin you've been talking about?" Cetan's friend just kept staring at me. Apparently he thought 'I wasn't going to be so beautiful.' Cetan quickly changed the subject and asked if we wanted to run with us after this game was done.

"Well duh! Who else do you know that can shoot like me bro?" I laughed. Cetan rolled his eyes. "Let's see it then," Cetan said matter of factly. We all sat and pulled out our basketball shoes from our school backpacks, tied our laces tight and took the floor. Cetan passed me the ball, then gave me that famous Native head nod as if to say,

"Shoot it." I didn't shoot it. I passed it to his friend. About 3 feet behind the arc this guy launches the ball with 2 people on him. I ran towards the basket in case I needed to rebound but I just heard the swish of the net. He pounds his head with two fists and runs backwards smiling at me. Cetan gives him a low five on the backcourt.

"Dreamer, I'll show you how to shoot like that." he says laughing. I roll my eyes. Cetan sees me roll my eyes and laughs. We won that game thanks to Bear Soldier (everyone just called him Bear).

A group of kids who were just spectating came over to us after the game. They all knew my cousin. Cetan was like that even as a young child. Other kids always wanted to be around him. This group of kids were the musicians and artists of the school. They all asked who I was, shook my hand, and said how pretty I was. That's the thing I loved. My peers. They did not know me as a person (yet), but they were so kind and so genuine. They complimented my beauty and made jokes that Cetan was no longer the best looking student in the school anymore. He would laugh at that statement, roll his eyes, and say things like, "Well Duh!" or "I told you, but you didn't believe me." or "Cut from the same cloth that's why." I loved it here.

    In my last class, twin sisters invited me to walk with them to the football field after school. It was a big rivalry game, and the sisters shared some of their favorite music with me as we walked to the field that day. They asked me what it was like being in a "white" school. I said it had its pros and cons. They knew not many Native kids went to the area public school. It was surprising to them that I stayed there for so many years. At that moment, I sort of regretted attending the public school because I always had to prove myself, always fighting to be seen no matter how hard I tried. Not here. Everyone loved me. Everyday peers I didn't know (yet) would call my name, "Dreamer in the house!" or "Dreamer, you good? What do you need?" My classmates were so friendly. They would buy me sodas and snacks from the vending machines. They would share their stories with me and we would all laugh. It felt so good to laugh. Sometimes we laugh so hard our eyes would fill with tears and no sound came out of our wide open mouths. And the best part. Unči was the school cook. Every Friday the entire school mauled the cafeteria for Unči's specialty-Chieftain chili. And her famous frybread of course.

The teachers at the tribal school were still mostly white, but they didn't roll their eyes when they saw me; they smiled and welcomed me into their classrooms. I remember being in shock when I heard the government teacher speak Lakota phrases of Lakota to the class before he started his government lesson. The first quarter went by and my grades were excellent. I qualified for the Talented & Gifted (TAG) Program, which the public school didn't have. This program helped me develop my interests and skills; I would take assessments to keep my mental capacity at peak performance for learning.

In May of my junior year, the students in the TAG program got to go on a trip to Hawaii. I was so excited because this would be the first time I ever flew on an airplane in my life, and we had landed on the Hawaiian shores on my golden birthday. It was a dream come true. I sat on that Hawiian beach reflecting on all the things I had experienced up to now. After so many years in a school where I fought everyday to be heard, to be accepted, here I was in Hawaii, laying on a beach with my pineapple drink listening to the waves glide along the sand and the seagulls mingling in the bright blue cloudless sky. It was the first time I actually felt appreciated as a student not having to work so hard just to be seen, just to feel like I was enough. I felt for the first time in my life the people at school genuinely loved and cared for me as a human being. I took a deep breath in, closed my eyes, and thanked the Creator for bringing me back to the Rez. To my people. And onto the Hawaiian Island of our Indigenous relatives. I am forever grateful to Lower Creek Tribal Schools for making me feel valued. Helping me remember that roots run deep. Reconnecting. Returning to the origins of what made our people so resilient and connected to one another and the world around us.

  Cousin Cetan had graduated after our trip to Hawaii. Bear (Soldier) and I were now the seniors. We became very close friends, and eventually started dating as high school students do. Honestly, it was scary to think this high school experience was going to end in a short nine months. Bear (Soldier) had a dream of becoming a college basketball player and saw himself taking home the championship trophy at the biggest Native basketball tournament not just on the Rez but in the state. He was so ambitious and funny. His laugh was contagious and I have never met a more kind hearted individual that he didn't have to be. Bear was raised by his Grandparents. He was so unique in every way-from his spirituality to the hardships he overcame in his life. I admired Bear. He had his own car, made his own money, and a positive outlook on life. He was charismatic and the Homecoming King, I the

Homecoming Queen. And we spent most of our time together.

High School on the Rez

The effects of oppression still existed on the Rez. As good as our school was, the generational trauma still lingered in the shadows. Some of my classmates struggled with their home lives. They struggled with not knowing any other way than that of their parents-alcohol, drugs, and for a few suicide was the only way out of the daily pain they experienced. A few miles from Unči's house, a boy a few years older than me that year took his own life. They called him "Paulie". I remember crying in my bed for nights on end, wishing this world was something else. Something different for my people. I started to see some of my classmates drinking with their families; it brought back memories of me as a child standing next to the kitchen table watching adults "throw back" cans and cans of beer.

It's different on the Rez as a teenager. You see the adults inviting the teenagers to the parties. Bear and I started to feel the heaviness of the Rez overwhelm our world. We started to go to the parties. The alcohol and drugs that I disowned and hated had entered my life. I didn't know why it was so easy to consume it all, but now for some reason the cycle of partying started to feel normal. I was living up to the term I heard the white people use, "Wild Indians." That's what we did, that's who we became. The regret still lingers within me. Of putting that poison into my body, into my mind. Something I will never forget is the hurt alcohol had caused Bear when he woke to the news of his best friend being killed in a drunk driving accident.

Pregnant and Alone

Not shortly after the passing of Bear's best friend, and despite being on birth control, I found out I was pregnant a few months into our Senior year. I was scared the night I shared the news with him, he was happy but still had an anxious look on his face. He held me tightly and told me everything would be okay. The weight of a new life hung on our shoulders as high schoolers.

The overwhelming grief of losing his best friend took hold of Bear. He looked so lost. He started to get high and we didn't have the same connection as before. I couldn't imagine what it was like to lose a best friend who I grew up with all my life. Bear and his best friend were inseparable. We originally both had plans of college basketball. As I sat in his car I overheard his friend ask if he was going to be a dad, he replied, "Shhhiiiiiii, no way...."

I felt my heart drop. I looked down at my growing belly, not quite yet noticeable for anyone to see. The love I thought I had was slipping through my fingers, and I was too tired to try to hold on.

Despite our son being born with a condition called craniosynostosis, we went our separate ways. Our son went through a skull surgery just when he was four months old. My son's head was the size of a melon, his eyes swollen shut, his cry barely loud enough to hear as the nurses rolled him out of the surgery room. My sister and my son's grandfather wept to see the pain he was experiencing, to see our baby on the brink of survival.

After the surgery, I moved in with my mother again and my son's father went on to become a successful college basketball player. I went on to be a college basketball dropout. I could no longer endure the 5 am practices, full day of classes, 3 hour evening practices, and staying up until 2 am trying to get homework done. All while my son was only 1 year old in daycare for long hours or with relatives while I did my best to juggle it all.

I continued my education, but traded basketball in for various jobs. Making beds in hotels, filing thousands of books at the university library, waitressing at the nearby highway truck stop, and cleaning multiple businesses at the midnight hour while my son slept. I learned to multitask the to-do list of life as my son and I trekked through it all alone. I remember strolling my son to the university library so I could pick up my work study check. It was about 5 miles from our apartment. I remember holding him in a bathroom stall while he cried to stay there before we made the long trek home. I had no car. But now I had enough money to get us food and bought us a couple tickets to the movie theater.

Fighting the Stereotype

A young, Indigenous single mother. I knew what they thought of me.

"They always end up like this."

"Another Rez girl with a baby."

"She had so much potential."

I heard the whispers. I saw the looks. They didn't see the late nights rocking my baby to sleep, the exhaustion that settled into my bones but never broke me. They didn't see the way I fought to stay in school, to keep going, to prove that I was more than they expected me to be. I refused to be their stereotype. I refused to be another sad story. Because I wasn't just fighting for myself anymore. I was fighting for my son. For the future I still believed I could have. For the love I knew I deserved.

Rising from the Ashes

Wówačhiŋ. (woe-wah-cheen—having determination and a strong will) That's what carried me through. Through the heartbreak. Through loneliness. Through the days when I wasn't sure how I was going to make it. But I did. I was more than the girl who had been hurt. I was more than the single mother they pitied. I was still Wihanblè S'a (Dreamer). And this was just the beginning of my story.

Chapter 5
Woman with a Chainsaw

I never thought I'd wield a chainsaw.

Not because I wasn't strong enough. Not because I wasn't willing. But because the world had already decided what I could and couldn't do. They saw me as a woman. A single mother. A Rez girl who should have stayed home, raising her baby, accepting whatever scraps life handed her. They did not see the fire in my eyes or the passion I held in my heart. They did not see the woman who would walk into the smoke, who would take the axe, who would stand shoulder to shoulder with men who thought she wouldn't last. But I knew something they didn't. I had already walked through flames before I ever stepped foot on the fireline. And I would not burn.

I just graduated college with my Bachelor's Degree in Education and became a Kindergarten Teacher. In the summers to make extra money, I signed up for wildland firefighting. Loving to hike and learning so many useful survival skills as a child, I knew I could apply those same skills out in the wilderness. I loved being in nature like when I was a little girl, just out in the open world of Grandmother Earth. From the Rocky Mountains to the Trails of Oregon, my team traveled across the country fighting fire wherever they needed us. One foggy morning, we had waited hours in our big green van while it rained. Some of the guys snoozed, but I couldn't take it anymore just sitting there. So, I jumped out of the van and picked up a huge boulder, held it over my head and started doing squats...in the rain...next to the red rock canyon with the flowing stream below. I was the only female on the squad and the boys in the van started smiling at one another. They had this look like, "What the heck is she doing?"

I didn't care. I loved smelling the rain that day, working my legs with that boulder, staying ready for the fire we were about to meet. The rain stopped. Our crew was able to drive up the fire road to start the work. Halfway up the hill we were stopped yet again in our big green van. So many things can happen on a fire detail; a semi carrying water had lost its breaks on the way down the hill and smashed into the side of the hill. Our crew heard the man driving the semi was badly injured so we all began to smudge and pray for the semi truck driver that day.

They boys and I reached the top of the plateau where we were to start "cutting line". Each of us grabbed our tool of choice and got in line ready to dig. I was good at digging line even when the fire was near and the smoke rolled in like a party fog machine.

"Dreamer, give up your tool. You're swamping today," my crew boss announced.

He was one of the highest class sawyers (someone who is trained to cut trees with a chainsaw) not just on our Rez, but all the Reservations in the country. My job that day was to gather all the tree stumps, logs, and shrubs he cut through and pile them all up in one place. All around me I heard the boys call, "TREE FALLING!" This was one of the safety protocols every sawyer had to call out. I realized this work was a different kind of hard. Just watching the boys walk up to a tree, assess its lean, get down on one knee and line up the chainsaw bar against the bark. They each had their own way to stay so focused. One of the guys would sing a Lakota song, another would make jokes and make everyone laugh. One of the main rules was to stay calm; I realized how important it was to stay calm when there are so many things going on around you. The boys "bucked up" the fallen trees into pieces. The stumps came in all different sizes and let me tell you, the squatting I did in the rain was just a measly warm up to the weight I carried in my hands. That was a good day's work. Good hard work. Dinner finally came and everyone was ready for their MRE meals. MRE meals were ready-to-eat survival meals. After a long day of cutting line, making jokes, enjoying the climb, those MRE meals were the next best thing to Unči's cooking. Man, how I miss those days!

    The next day we continued to acclimate our bodies at a ski resort to adjust being 12,000 feet in the air in the Rocky Mountains. After a few hours and some team physical training, we got in line and trekked. "ROCK!" the squad line leader said, following in unison the line shouts "ROCK!" to let everyone know a big rock is in the path of our trek. The 90 percent incline and thinner air begins to take a toll on our breaths. The oldest guy on our team started to get a bloody nose, so we took a short break. Our squad boss looked at him in disappointment because the head fire supervisors were always watching us-the "Indian fire crew". If we didn't perform up to their standard they could send us back home. Our crew leader looked every single one of us in the eye and told us to find our strength...and so we did.

The Fireline Brotherhood

There were no half-measures in firefighting. You either carried your weight, or you were dead weight. And I refused to be dead weight. My crew was made up of men hardened by years of back-breaking work, sweat-stained bandanas wrapped around their foreheads, muscles carved by the mountains they had conquered. They had no time for weakness. And in the beginning, they weren't sure what to make of me.

"She won't last," I overheard one of them say. "It's too dangerous for her."

I wanted to tell them I had already survived dangers they couldn't even imagine. But I didn't waste my breath. I let my work speak for me. Wrapping my small wrists with tape to help me sturdy the saw, I cut all day alongside them. I ran with the squad up the steepest inclines, my lungs burning, my boots digging into the loose earth. I swung the Pulaski, my hands blistering, my arms screaming for rest. I hoisted logs heavier than my own body, cleared debris with the same relentless determination as the men beside me. And little by little, the doubt in their eyes was replaced with something else. Respect. I wasn't their little sister. I wasn't a fragile thing they had to babysit. I was one of them.

I felt the presence of the Creator once we reached the top of that peak. Rocky Mountain snow crunching underneath my boots, I stood there looking out at the glorious view of hunter green peaks all around me. I closed my eyes, felt Tatè (the wind) gentle on my face, the sun beaming on my shoulders. I spoke my prayers softly to the Creator and whispered how grateful I was to be alive in that moment. After climbing mountains with "my boys", and sleeping on the solid ground for two weeks, we headed back to the Rez, back home.

After we got home and back to our fire agency, I kept helping the sawyers with the swamping work. Then it happened. I would have never imagined myself picking up a chainsaw, let alone knowing how to use one. The first time I held a chainsaw, I could feel the weight of it in my hands—not just the steel and the power but the expectation that I couldn't handle it.

"I don't know, boss, you think she can even carry it for a whole day?"

I was young. A single mom. A woman. And in the world of wildland firefighting, that made me an outsider before I even stepped onto the line. But I was never one to back down.

Fire and Fury

I started going with the boys to the fire shed where they housed all the chainsaw equipment, and some of them looked at me, shook their heads and laughed under their breath. Some of them thought I was just being picked to go because I was good looking and the boss had a crush on me.

"You? On a fire crew?"

"It's dangerous out there."

"Shouldn't you be at home with your baby?"

The doubt was only more fuel to my fire. I had spent my whole life proving people wrong—why should this be any different? I needed the job, the paycheck, the chance to do something that made me feel alive. I wanted to show my son that his mother was strong, that she could take on anything. If that meant running toward the raging fire instead of away from it, that is exactly what I was meant to do. There was no room for fear, only the notion that a young single mother as petite as I was could stand amongst the strongest of men.

Earning My Place

The first days were tough. Some of the men on the crew weren't cruel, but they weren't exactly welcoming either. They didn't say it outright, but I knew what they were thinking: She won't last. She's just a distraction.

I not only pushed through the grueling physical training I fell in love with it. The long hikes with heavy packs, the relentless heat, the exhaustion that settled deep in my muscles. I ignored the blisters on my feet and the ache in my back. I didn't just want to keep up—I wanted to be better. Then came the real test: the chainsaw.

It wasn't just about cutting trees. It was about control, precision, respect for the machine in your hands. It was about knowing when to let the saw work and when to force it, about listening to the sound of the engine and feeling the vibration in your grip. The first time I pulled the cord and felt the engine roar to life, I knew—I belonged here.

Breaking Another Stereotype

I wasn't supposed to be there. Not as an Indigenous woman. Not as a single mom. Firefighting was for men, for the ones who were expected to be strong, to be fearless. But what they didn't understand was that I had already survived things worse than fire.

I had already walked through the flames of heartbreak, of struggle, of proving my worth again and again. The fire didn't scare me. I took down trees as thick as my torso, felt the sawdust stick to my sweat-covered skin, breathed in the scent of pine and smoke. I held my own in a world that wasn't built for me. The fear I felt from seeing my relatives fight, feeling all alone in this world raising my son, letting go of men who tried to control me all dissipated in those moments I cut through brush making a way, a new way for myself. When the crew saw that I wasn't backing down and saw what I could do, something shifted. The looks changed from doubt to respect. I had earned my place.

Lessons in the Ashes

Fire is destruction, but it is also renewal. It clears the deadwood, makes way for new growth. I felt that same fire in me. With every tree I cut, with every step I took into the smoke and heat, I felt the old version of myself burning away. The girl who doubted her worth. The girl who let others define her. What remained was something stronger. I wasn't just a single mother. I wasn't just a rez girl. I wasn't just a woman in a man's world. I was a firefighter. I was a sawyer. A survivor. A warrior. Living my summers among the raging fires had only made me stronger.

Chapter 6
Finding My Identity

Fire doesn't stay in one place. It moves. It spreads. It follows the wind, searching for something to consume, something to transform. And like fire, I traveled across the land that bore me—leaving behind the ashes of a past I could no longer survive in, carrying the embers of a future I refused to let burn out. For myself. For my son. But no matter how far I ran, the scars of what I had endured burned beneath my skin. I had survived many things. Poverty. Judgment. The exhaustion of being a single mother, balancing college, work, and a sport meant for those without mouths to feed. But what I hadn't escaped—what followed me like a shadow, growing darker with time—was the weight of an abusive relationship. A man who claimed to love me, yet used his words to threaten and hands to silence me. A man who wrapped his anger around my throat like a leash, pulling tighter every time I tried to leave. While my son was away with his father, I encountered a night I didn't think I would survive. Alcohol consumed bodies, flashes of me gasping for a breath to scream for help still haunts me; waking up on Easter to the ravage my neck endured that night. A man who said he needed me, but never enough to change. I told myself it would get better. That maybe if I was stronger, softer, more patient—it would stop. Every allegation was an ember pressed into my skin, each cruel word a gust of wind fueling the flames that threatened to consume me. After fighting for my life, his hands like a noose around my throat, the fire within me dimmed to embers. Love had become a shadow, and I walked through a world that felt cold and colorless. But even in the ashes, something stirred—a quiet spark, stubborn and sacred. With time, breath returned, the fire reignited, and I began to rise—not as I was, but stronger, forged by the very flames meant to destroy me. I saw how it affected my son. The one person I was meant to protect.

My son was so intelligent, funny, and deeply caring. He was outgoing, hoop danced in front of large crowds, sang loudly without fear of retribution, and spoke up for himself. Unči and Ína said he had an old soul. After witnessing the fighting he stopped laughing as much. He started looking away when I spoke, like it hurt to see me. And then, one night, after another fight that left my body aching and my spirit frayed, he broke.

"Mom," he whispered, his voice hoarse from the weight of words he had been too afraid to say. "Can we leave? Please leave him mom."

I looked at him—really *looked* at him—and saw it. The pain in his eyes of all that he had witnessed. It was in his heart. In his mind. He had seen too much. Felt too much. And it was breaking him. The one thing I swore I would never allow myself to fall into was consuming my life and that of my son. That was my breaking point. I would not let my son continue to witness the violence that I said I would never experience.

Traveling to a New Land

We left. My son and I spread across the plains life a fire. We moved away from the Rez I thought was home. Away from a man who had stolen too many years of our lives. I carried my son with me, my hands steady as I gathered what was left of our lives and placed them in a new place, a new land, a new Rez that held something I had never had before—*a future.* Here, there was a university. A chance to earn my Master's degree. A chance to build something that couldn't be taken from me. A chance to show my son that *leaving was not giving up.* It was survival. It was the first step toward healing.

The Truth in the Old Ways

For so long, I had felt like I was drifting between two worlds. The one I had been raised in—where my blood, my language, my history were all things the outside world tried to erase. And the one I had been forced into—where success meant leaving behind the ways of my ancestors, assimilating into a system never meant for us. But in this new place, I found something different. I found the people Unči had spoken of. The healers. The ones who still carried the songs in their throats, the prayers in their palms, the medicine in their hearts. They were not stories. They were real. And they had never left.

I sat in ceremony for the first time, the scent of wáhpé (wahḵ-pay, wild bergamot) in my palms as I rubbed them together, thinking, praying. The drum pounded steady, and I felt my heartbeat match its tune. Watching this healer load his čanupa (cha-noo-pa, sacred pipe) while the voices of the singers enticed me to join in. In the complete darkness of the room I felt whole again. For the first time in my life, I did not feel like I was standing between two worlds. I *was* the world. I was Lakota.

Eyes closed, images entered my mind, not by my imagination but by something older—ancestral, alive. They rose like smoke, curling through time, revealing a young girl who had once been lost in silence and survival. She looked like me. She *was* me. I saw my son's face, too—his eyes searching mine, asking if we were safe now. I saw the children I taught, their laughter like prayers carried on the wind. In that dark room, lit only by the sound of the drum and the scent of wáhpé, I knew: I had survived for them. I had returned to remember who I was—not just a woman rebuilt by fire, but a mother, a teacher, a Lakota woman called to help others remember their own light. I was not between two worlds. I was the world. I *am* Lakota. And I am still here. We hold the sacred blood of the women who had come before us. The warriors who had fought to keep our people alive, who had carried babies on their backs while running from soldiers who wanted us dead. I was the granddaughter of a woman who had been beaten for speaking her language—*and I would never let it be silenced again.* I was the mother of a boy who deserved more than the pain of the past—*and I would give him a new future.* I was *fire.* Not the kind that destroyed. The kind that cleansed. That made way for new growth. That turned the old into something stronger, something unbreakable. And from that moment on, I would never let my flame go out again.

Chapter 7
Teacher Life

I never planned on becoming a teacher. As a child, school had been both a sanctuary and a battlefield—a place where I thrived academically but also had to fight to prove I belonged. I saw how Native kids were treated differently, how expectations for us were set lower, how our history was rewritten or erased altogether. Still, I loved to learn. I soaked up knowledge like a sponge, eager to prove that I was more than what people assumed about a "Rez girl." But back then, I never thought I would one day stand at the front of a classroom.

It wasn't until I had my son as a teenager that I realized the need for me to learn early childhood and adolescent development so that I could be a good mother. It wasn't until I saw the world through their eyes, that I realized just how much our kids *needed* someone who understood them—someone who believed in them the way they deserved. That's when I knew our kids needed someone that looked like them in the classroom. Someone who knew what it was like growing up on the Rez. I had to become an educator.

More Than a Job, A Calling

Becoming a teacher wasn't just about lesson plans and textbooks. It was about fighting for our kids in a system that wasn't built for them. It was about making sure the next generation didn't have to feel invisible in their own classrooms. I didn't want my students to go through what I had gone through—being the only Native kid in a room full of white faces, feeling like an outsider in a school meant to educate all children. I didn't want them to be labeled as "at risk" just because they came from the Reservation. I didn't want them to feel like they had to work twice as hard just to be seen. So I made a promise to myself: In my classroom, every child would know they were valued. Their voices would matter. Their stories would be told.

Lakota Identity In Education

One of the hardest things about growing up in the school system was realizing how little of my own history was being taught. I learned about Christopher Columbus before I learned about my own ancestors. I read about the Declaration of Independence before I ever heard the stories of our treaties, the ones that were broken time and time again. I knew more about the Boston Tea Party than I did about Wounded Knee.

That was unacceptable. When I stepped into my first classroom as a teacher, I knew things had to change. I made sure my students saw themselves in their education.

We spoke Lakota words, even if just a few at a time. One of my first teaching experiences was being a long term substitute teacher for a high school Indian Studies class. We read The Journey of Crazy Horse by Sicangu author Joseph Marshall III. My students heard of Crazy Horse but never knew the courage he displayed long ago. I told them we have the same blood running through our veins; we can do courageous things too. We watched videos about our origin stories of star knowledge and sacred sites. We learned our true history—the strength of our people, not just the suffering. We celebrated our traditions, our values, our way of life. And for the first time, I saw something shift in my students. They sat up straighter. They asked more questions. They felt pride in who they were, instead of feeling like they had to hide it. Because representation matters. When our kids see themselves in the lessons they learn, they start to believe they belong in the future being built around them.

Advocating for Our Wakanyeja

But teaching wasn't just about what happened inside the classroom. It was about fighting for my students outside of it, too. I saw kids come to school hungry, unable to focus because their last meal had been the school lunch the day before. I saw kids struggling with trauma, with violence at home, with burdens no child should have to carry. I saw students who had been told—by teachers, by the system, by the world—that they weren't meant to succeed. I refused to let that stand. I advocated for resources, for programs that supported our kids beyond academics. I worked with other incredible Indigenous educators to make sure our school wasn't just a place to learn—it was a place to be safe, to be heard, to be empowered. We sent food bags home every weekend so students could have something to eat at home. I realized then that being an educator wasn't just about teaching. It was about protecting. It was about uplifting. It was about making sure no child ever felt alone in their fight to succeed.

Teaching Against the Odds

Every morning, my students arrived carrying more than just backpacks. Some carried hunger, their stomachs empty from a home that couldn't afford breakfast. Some carried exhaustion, their nights spent listening to arguments, to the echoes of generational pain playing out in real-time. Others carried the burden of self-doubt, of being told—by teachers before me, by society, by their own circumstances—that they weren't meant for success.

I had students who showed up late, not because they didn't care, but because they had to help their younger siblings get ready while their parents worked or struggled with addiction. I had students who put their heads down on their desks, not because they were lazy, but because sleep wasn't something they had the privilege of getting. And yet, they were there. That, in itself, was resilience. But resilience shouldn't have to be their only survival skill.

Fighting Stereotypes in Education

I quickly learned that the biggest battles in education weren't just about funding or policies. They were about perception. I sat in meetings where students were labeled "troubled" simply because they were Native. Where their struggles were seen as inevitable, their potential dismissed before they even had a chance to prove themselves.

"They come from broken homes."

"They don't care about school."

"They'll just drop out anyway."

I've heard those words too many times—spoken like truths, but rooted in ignorance. Every time, I think of that little Rez girl I used to be, how adults looked at me and saw a statistic instead of a story. They had already decided who I'd become, before I ever had the chance to show them who I was. I knew the truth—our kids do care. They are smart. They are capable. They have dreams just like any other children. They just need someone to believe in them, someone to push back against the expectations that have been placed on them for generations. I made sure they knew. I told them they were brilliant. That they could be anything they wanted to be. That their history did not define their future, but their strength did. I told them they were geniuses because I knew how much I had needed to hear those words when I was their age.

When Teaching Meant Healing

There were days I left school feeling helpless, the weight of my students' stories pressing down on me. The child who flinched when someone raised their voice, because home wasn't a safe place. The student who couldn't focus because they were worrying about where they'd sleep that night. The girl who reminded me of myself—bright, full of potential, but slowly dimming under the pressures of being "different." I wanted to fix everything. What could I do? I stayed consistent. I stayed being the teacher who didn't give up on them. The one who saw past the anger, the silence, the resistance—and recognized the pain underneath. I advocated for them in the best ways I knew how. I worked to create safe spaces where students could talk, where they could breathe. I spoke their names with love and pride, reminding them every day that they mattered. For so many of them, school wasn't just a place to learn. School was a place of stability and safety. It was their refuge.

Beyond the Classroom Walls

The challenges of education didn't stop at the school doors. The Reservation itself was struggling. Poverty, lack of resources, historical trauma—it all bled into the classroom, shaping the futures of children before they even had a chance to write their own stories. I saw brilliant students drop out because they had to work to support their families. I saw talented athletes miss opportunities because transportation to games and practices was unreliable. I saw future doctors, artists, and leaders lose hope because no one ever told them that their dreams were possible. And I knew that if real change was going to happen, it had to go beyond the classroom. I fought for policies that supported Indigenous students. I pushed for more representation in the curriculum, for programs that connected students to their culture rather than erasing it. I worked to bring in community members, elders, mentors—people who could show our kids that success didn't have to mean leaving the

Rez, that they could thrive while staying connected to their roots. Because education isn't just about grades. It's about empowerment. If we want our children to succeed, we have to give them more than just knowledge. We have to give them belief—in themselves, in their culture, in the future that belongs to them.

There are still days that break my heart. Days when I lose a student to the same cycles I've spent my career trying to fight. Days when I wonder if I'm making enough of a difference. Days when I feel like I'm pushing against a wall that refuses to move. But then I see a student who once struggled walk across the graduation stage, their cap decorated with Lakota symbols. I see a child who once doubted their worth stand up in class and speak their truth with confidence. I see the next generation rising, reclaiming their power, proving that they are more than the challenges placed before them. The fight for our children isn't just about them. It's about all of us. And as long as I have a voice, as long as I have the strength to stand, I will keep advocating for them. For their futures. For their dreams. For the world they deserve to live in. Because they are worth it. They have always been worth it.

From Teacher to Leader

The more I worked in education, the more I saw the barriers our kids faced. The more I saw those barriers, the more I knew I had to do more than just teach. I had to create much needed change outside the walls of the classroom. Stepping into a leadership role wasn't easy. As a young Indigenous woman, I had to fight to be taken seriously, to be heard in rooms where decisions were being made for our children without our voices. Because if I didn't, who would? Becoming a principal wasn't just about career advancement. It was about ensuring that change wasn't just happening in my classroom, but throughout the entire school. It was about making sure our students were surrounded by people who believed in them, who saw their potential, who refused to let them be statistics. Even now, the fight isn't over.

Every day, I walk into my school knowing that I carry the weight of something bigger than myself. The dreams of our ancestors. The hopes of our future generations. The responsibility to keep pushing forward, no matter how hard it gets. Our children deserve better. They deserve to see themselves as leaders, as doctors, as artists, as storytellers. They deserve a world that doesn't try to erase them, but instead lifts them up. I will spend my entire career making sure they get exactly that. I am more than just an educator. I am a warrior for the future of my people. And I will never stop fighting for them. Being an educator on the Rez isn't just about teaching. It's about understanding. About meeting children where they are, knowing what they carry with them when they walk through the school doors. It's about balancing lesson plans with real-life struggles, about being more than just a teacher—being a protector, an advocate, a voice for those who haven't yet found their own. I knew this journey wouldn't be easy. I knew our children faced obstacles far beyond missing homework assignments or low test scores. Sometimes nothing can prepare you for the weight of what you witness, the heartbreak of seeing young spirits dimmed by the world around them.

Chapter 8

Leadership

I never dreamed of being a school leader. But life has a way of preparing you for things before you even realize it. Every battle I had fought—the endless training to just be seen in sports, the long nights of single motherhood, the exhaustion of college, the bruises I had hidden, the firelines I had walked, the classrooms where I had fought for my students—had shaped me into something unbreakable. When the opportunity came to step up, I didn't hesitate. I knew our wakáŋyeja deserved more—more than survival, more than what this world was willing to give. If no one else would fight for them, then I would. With every breath, every step, every prayer—I would stand for them, because they are the future of our Oyáte.

Sitting behind that principal's desk for the first time, I felt the weight of it settle into my bones. The job wasn't just about test scores and schedules. It was about children who came to school hungry because their pantries were empty. It was about families who didn't trust the system because the system had failed them for generations. It was about teachers who wanted to make a difference but were drowning in red tape, low pay, and outdated curriculums. For me, it was about reclaiming the narrative—because I remember being that little Rez girl, sitting in classrooms where no one saw me, where my story didn't seem to belong. Now, as a principal, I carry that memory with me—not as a wound, but as a promise. I knew our children deserve better, and I knew our community held the strength to give it to them. This wasn't a journey I could walk alone. It takes all of us—families, elders, teachers, and the children themselves—to turn our schools from places of survival into places of thriving. Together, we are restoring what was broken. We're bringing back what was always ours: a way of learning rooted in love, culture, and connection. This work is about healing, yes—but it's also about rising together, so the next generation can walk a little taller, knowing exactly who they are and where they come from.

Being a principal on the Rez meant enduring battles most school leaders never had to think about. I pushed back against policies, refusing to let our children be afterthoughts. I fought for resources that schools off the Rez took for granted—clean ventilation in mouse ridden trailers, updated science and math curriculum, technology, mental health support, and books that were written by Indigenous authors so students can aspire to be one. I strove for every opportunity our kids *deserved*. I demanded more than the watered-down version of history the state tried to feed our children. I continue to fight for our language to rise like a ceremonial song within the walls of our school, for our culture to be woven into every story, every step, and for our children to look into their learning and see their reflection—whole, proud, and rooted in who they are. I don't fight alone. I am building a team of teachers, staff, and community members who share the same vision:. It's about setting the system itself aflame, burning away the structures that bound us, and from the ashes, forging a new way—one that allows for transformation and rebirth. Our children should no longer have to code-switch, to hide who they are or shrink to fit in. Instead, they should enter schools as their whole selves—rooted in their culture, their language, and their truth—and be celebrated for it.

The Children Keep Me Going

Some days, the strife felt endless. The paperwork. The meetings. The pushback from people who wanted things to stay the same. But then, I'd step into the classrooms and see the reason I kept going. The little girl who proudly introduced herself in Lakota, her voice steady, unafraid. The boy who had struggled with reading but now stayed after school, determined to improve. The student who pulled me aside and whispered,

"Miss Dreamer, I want to be like you. You are the best principal ever," or "Miss Dreamer, can I stay at this school forever?" Those moments reminded me—change wasn't immediate. But it was happening. One student at a time.

Breaking Cycles, Building Futures

Education had been used as a weapon against our people for generations. Boarding schools had tried to erase us. Public schools had ignored us. But we were still here. Now, we reclaim education—not as a tool of oppression, but as a path to freedom. We teach our language, our history, our ways. We are raising leaders who can go beyond the Rez, armed with knowledge and pride. We are breaking the cycles of poverty, of hopelessness, of believing we were less than. This fight isn't just about me. It is about every Indigenous child who walks through our school doors, carrying the weight of history on their shoulders. I will carry that weight with them—until the day they no longer have to.

Chapter 9

A Journey of Revival

Imagine this: the sun is still a whisper on the horizon, the air thick with the promise of a new day. Before dawn breaks, we rise—eyes tired, spirit heavy with the weight of the world, but you step forward with purpose. The earth beneath you is cool, damp with morning dew, and you can feel the energy of wakiksuyé (those that have passed on), their footsteps still pressed into the soil.

The Sundance ceremony was born from a place of deep connection to the land, the spirits, and the sacred forces that guide us. It is a ceremony of renewal, sacrifice, and prayer—a way to connect with the Creator and to offer something of ourselves in exchange for the healing of our people, the land, and the future. Traditionally, Sundance was a men's ceremony, where men would undergo physical trials, fasting, and dance to honor the Čháŋ Wakȟaŋ (chon wokon-sacred tree) at the center of the circle, to offer prayers. As a woman, I was called to endure—my naġi (spirit) drawn not out of obligation, but out of a need to connect, to sacrifice, to be part of something larger than myself. I felt the fire of my ancestors burning within me, a fire that could not be ignored. Čháŋ Wakȟaŋ became a symbol of renewal for me—a living, breathing embodiment of rebirth. Just as fire consumes the old to give birth to the new, I danced, enduring the heat and the suffering, knowing that each moment of sacrifice would be a step toward my own renewal.

Together, we moved as one, each of us connected by a spirit older than time. Feet pounding the earth, hands raised to the sky, every step, every movement a prayer, the tree in the center our anchor. This sacred being standing tall as it takes the heaviness from our minds. In its glorious presence, our bodies embracing the elements, our heartbeats in sync with the drum.

From dawn to dusk, for four days, we dance with no food or water, our bodies tested in the blistering heat of summer. As the sun rises higher, we continue on, dancing, still praying. Sweat no longer pours down. The weight of the prayers we carry, the hopes for our families, our people, and our children at the forefront of our being. We dance for the future, for the healing of our communities, and for the generations to come.

When evening comes, we pause—exhausted, drained, but not defeated. We are stronger for the suffering, stronger for the prayers whispered with every step. Our bodies have been emptied, yet we are filled with something deeper than hunger or thirst. We are filled with spirit. We are filled with the strength of those who danced before us and those who will come after us. Like the flames that purify and renew, we are reborn through our endurance. In the heat of the (Wíwáng Wači) Sundance circle, we shed the old, broken parts that no longer serve us. We rise stronger, more connected to our ancestors, and continue to ignite the fire within us.

As I continued to walk through life, I found that true healing wasn't just in surviving the battles I had faced—it was in learning to *live* in balance, in alignment with the teachings of my ancestors. My journey wasn't only about my life as a little Rez girl, a mother, or a teacher leader; it was about reconnecting with the heartbeat of our Lakota traditions, reviving the sacred practices that had been passed down through generations.

When my second son was born, I didn't expect the pain that would follow. My C-section, necessary for his safe arrival, left me broken in ways I never imagined. My body, wounded and in agony, felt foreign to me. Every time I tried to gather my baby close, I was met with a sharp reminder of how fragile I had become. I couldn't fully embrace him, my baby I had longed for, the way my spirit had hoped. It was in this moment of deep pain—physical and emotional—that I turned to the local spiritual leader for healing. I was taught how to properly ask for healing by offering my čanupa- this is called an obaġi. I needed physical recovery and a restoration of spirit. In the ceremony I was given péjuta (medicine) and healed by the spirits.

Inípi (sweat lodge) is a place where my body and spirit can be cleansed, where I can shed the weight of pain and sorrow. The heat, the steam, the prayers—they all are a way to breathe life back into me. Each time I entered that sacred space, I felt my body soften, the tension easing with every breath, as the steam swirled around me like the loving embrace of Unči, who recently made her journey back to the stars...

The heat purges my spirit of what it no longer needs—anger, shame, fear. The heat of the lodge reminds me that even in my vulnerability, I was strong. Through each ceremony, I learned to embrace my body again—not as broken or weak, but as the vessel that carried my son, the vessel that endured pain to bring him into this world. I began to heal not just from the wound on my abdomen, but from the pain of not being able to fully connect with him in the way I had hoped. I continue to learn the value of sacrifice, the importance of surrendering to something greater than myself. Fasting, dancing, and praying—each step in the ceremony was a reminder that healing comes not only through our physical bodies but through our spirits as well. Sundance taught me that endurance is sacred, that we carry the strength of generations within us, and that our suffering is not in vain—it has a purpose, it teaches us resilience.

In the quiet of the morning, when the world is still, I hold my čanupa (sacred pipe) in my hands. I offer my prayers, remembering Unči, my family, my sons, my healing, and the future that I work to build for myself. Each prayer is a step toward healing the wounds both seen and unseen that had once defined me. It was as if every word of my prayer was a stitch in the fabric of my soul, mending the parts of me that had been torn apart. I began to feel my connection to my ancestors, to the land, to the teachings of my people. I was not broken; I was being rebuilt, piece by piece, from the inside out. I no longer felt divided between two worlds. The teachings of my culture, once buried beneath the weight of colonialism, were alive once more in my heart, mind, and spirit. Through my own healing, I can help heal the next generation. The journey hasn't been easy, but it is mine to walk—and with every step, I can bring our Lakota ways back into the light.

Unčičila's

My Dear Grandmother's

Chapter 10

The Future

They tried to erase us. Through massacres, through forced removals, through boarding schools that tore our children from our arms. Through policies that stripped us of our language, our land, our identity. They wrote about us in history books as if we were ghosts, as if we were gone. But we are *still here.* Now, we are speaking. Now, we are fighting. Now, we are calling on the world to listen to the stories that lay underneath every single story created in America. As you hold this book in your hands, you are holding the stories of every Indigenous child who has ever been told they are less than. You are holding the weight of history that tried to break us. You are holding an ember that when sprinkled with cedar, azílya's (uh-zeel-iah-smudges) the spirit. Now, I ask you, dearest reader: **What will you do with it?** Will you look away, the way the world has looked away from us for centuries? Or will you stand to make a difference in the lives of the original inhabitants of this land? Our children are still here. They are waking up in homes where hunger gnaws at their bellies before the school bell even rings. They are sitting in classrooms that don't reflect their faces, their stories, their strength. They are fighting battles no child should have to fight—poverty, addiction, suicide rates that are the highest in the nation. They deserve better. And they cannot do this alone.

The Key to Our Future

For too long, education was used as a weapon against us. Boarding schools stripped our children of their identities, their names, their language. Public schools erased our history, teaching generations of Native and non-Native children alike that we were nothing more than a tragic footnote. But now, we reclaim education as our greatest weapon of *resistance*. Our children must see themselves in their curriculum—not just as victims, but as warriors, as innovators, as leaders. Our schools must be places of healing, not trauma—where teachers understand the weight our students carry and help them rise above it. Our youth must know that education is not about leaving the Rez behind—it is about returning stronger, armed with knowledge and power.

I have spent my life walking through flames. As a young girl, proving I was more than the stereotypes placed upon me. As a mother, ensuring my children would grow up knowing their worth. As an educator, breaking the cycles that have held my people down for too long. But my fire is not just mine. It belongs to the next generation. And it belongs to you. This is not just my fight. This is a fight for every

Indigenous child who still dreams, despite the odds stacked against them. This is a fight for every ancestor who survived so we could be here today. This is a fight for the future. If you have read this far, you may already be part of this story. I ask you, help us be heard:

✦ **Advocate for Indigenous education.** Demand that our history, our voices, and our languages are taught in every school, not just on Reservations.

✦ **Support Indigenous educators and leaders.** We are here, doing the work—but we need allies who will stand beside us.

✦ **Listen to Indigenous voices.** Read our stories. Share our struggles. Amplify our successes. We are not relics of the past—we are thriving, evolving, and shaping the future.

- **Fight for our children.** They deserve the same opportunities, the same resources, the same belief in their potential as any other child in this country.

This is not just an Indigenous fight. This is a human fight. A fight for justice. A fight for truth. A fight for a future where our children are no longer seen as a statistic, but as the leaders they were born to be. They tried to silence us. They tried to bury our voices beneath centuries of oppression. But as with fire, the harder you try, the brighter and stronger it burns. I—along with my people, my children, my students, my ancestors—am still lighting the way. Still rising. Still fighting. Still here. Because the fire is not just mine anymore. It belongs to you, too. The fire within us all to make a better life for the future of humanity. We are not victims, we are warriors. Let's rise and thrive together.

Epilogue
The Fire Stays Lit

The fire has never gone out. Not in me. Not in my people. Not in the children who walk these lands, carrying the strength of generations in their blood. I used to think survival was enough—to make it out, to prove the world wrong, to break through the barriers set before me. But survival isn't the final goal. We are meant for more than just getting by. We are meant to thrive and live a life full of purpose.

Looking back, I see the winding road that led me here—the hardships, the victories, the moments I thought I wouldn't make it. Every challenge shaped me, sharpened me, prepared me to stand where I am today. I've seen the darkest parts of our reality—the violence, the addiction, the way history has tried to break us again and again. But I have also seen the light. I've seen children who were once counted out rise up and take back their power. I've seen families reconnect with their language, their culture, their pride. I've seen our people reclaim their stories, refusing to be defined by the pain of the past. And I know now—our fire is unstoppable.

Memoirs of a Rez Girl

Study Guide

This study guide is designed to accompany "Memoirs of a Rez Girl" by Leslie Crow. It provides discussion questions, reflection prompts, and action steps to deepen readers' engagement with the book. Whether used in classrooms, book clubs, or personal study, this guide encourages critical thinking, self-reflection, and advocacy.

CHAPTER DISCUSSION QUESTIONS

Prologue: The Fire Within

1. How does the Author use fire as a metaphor for her life?
2. What does the opening scene tell us about Dreamer's resilience?

Chapter 1: Born of the Land

1. How does the Author describe her connection to the land?
2. What role does her Unči play in shaping her identity?

Chapter 2: Born of Ína

1. What challenges does Dreamer face as one of the few Native students in her school?
2. What kind of impact does her mother attending college have on her?

Chapter 3-10: Reread your favorite parts of each chapter 3-10 and envision yourself in that moment. For each chapter pick out a sentence or phrase that resonated with you. How does the statement you chose make you feel? Why does this statement resonate with you?

REFLECTION & WRITING PROMPTS

1. Dreamer faces many obstacles in her journey. Write about a time when you overcame a significant challenge.
2. What does fire symbolize in <u>Memoirs of a Rez Girl</u>? How does this metaphor evolve throughout the book?
3. If you could ask the author one question about her experiences, what would it be and why?

TAKING ACTION

Memoirs of a Rez Girl is not just a story of survival—it is a call to action. Here are ways you can support Indigenous education and advocacy:

• Learn about Indigenous history from Native voices.
• Donate to organizations that provide resources for Indigenous students.
• Amplify Indigenous voices by sharing their stories, books, and activism.

Acknowledgements

Thank you toÍna (my Mother) for the incredible support in helping me build up the courage to write this book. Your own story of courage has helped me in my everyday life. A special thank you to my family for always believing in me and taking care of the little things at home as I worked on this book. Additionally, a huge shout out to all my students, all the incredible educators I had the honor to work beside, and my fire squad that helped mold me into who I am today. Lastly, I say wópíla tánka (woh-pee-lah tonk-ah, thank you so very much) to Unči for instilling in me loving kindness and strength alike to help me on this journey... So far...

www.ingramcontent.com/pod-product-compliance
Lightning Source LLC
Chambersburg PA
CBHW060348190426
43201CB00043B/1762